Rumi

GARDENS OF THE BELOVED

Other titles by the same authors

Whispers of the Beloved
Hidden Music

Rumi

GARDENS OF THE BELOVED

Translated by

Maryam Mafi and Azima Melita Kolin

JUN 2004

Element
An Imprint of HarperCollins*Publishers*
77–85 Fulham Palace Road,
Hammersmith, London W6 8JB

The website address is: www.thorsonselement.com

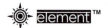

and *Element* are trademarks of
HarperCollins*Publishers* Ltd

First published by Element 2003

1 3 5 7 9 10 8 6 4 2

Text copyright © Maryam Mafi and Azima Melita Kolin 2003

Source: Koliyat-e Divan Shams Tabrizi, Badi al-Zaman Forouzanfar,
Tehran: Amir Kabir Publishers, 1336/1957

Book cover design: Azima Melita Kolin
Calligraphy: Ali Tasharofi
Editor: Kim Richardson
Co-ordinator for the calligraphy: Bahman Bayani

Maryam Mafi and Azima Melita Kolin assert the
moral right to be identified as the authors of this work

A catalogue record of this book
is available from the British Library

ISBN 0 00 717073 4

Printed and bound in Great Britain by
Creative Print and Design Wales

Contents

Introduction

Rumi – Mowlana Jalaludin Mohamad – one of the most revered mystical poets of all times, was born on 30 September 1207 in Balkh. As the Mogul invasion of the Persian Empire drew near, Rumi and his family moved to Konya in Turkey, where he lived until his death on 17 December 1273. A descendant of a long line of Islamic scholars, Rumi was educated in the Sufi tradition by his father and his followers. Upon his father's death, Rumi, still in his early twenties, took over the position as head of the theological school in Konya, which had been specifically created for his father by the local ruler. He excelled in all theological fields and acquired many devoted followers.

In 1244 Rumi met Shams of Tabriz, a wandering dervish and a highly advanced spiritual master, who set fire to Rumi's heart and revealed to him the direct path to the Beloved. The intensity of their encounter led to Rumi's forsaking his school and students, which resulted in great resentment on their part.

Shams and Rumi did not have much time together – perhaps only two-and-a-half years – before Shams disappeared from Rumi's life. Some say Shams was murdered by Rumi's jealous followers; some believe that he left because he knew he could teach Rumi nothing more. After Shams' disappearance Rumi, in search of his ultimate Beloved, turned to poetry to express the pain of his loss; he became a lover, a poet par excellence, a dervish, a mystic. No one has ever understood who was the student and who was the master.

Rumi's colossal volume, *Divan of Shams of Tabriz*, contains 3500 odes and almost 2000 quatrains. His monumental *Masnavi* is a six-volume treasury of teaching poems, containing over 25,000 verses in which he uses the media of story, tale and anecdote to explore the multifaceted layers of spiritual wisdom. His *Fi ma Fihi*, or *Discourses*, gathered into a book by his followers after his death, is a collection of lectures, comments, sermons and conversations on a variety of subjects directly affecting the everyday life of man and his relationship with the divine.

Gardens appear in many of Rumi's poems; they are symbols depicting the inner spaces of the soul, heart and spirit. Sometimes the poems take us through gardens filled with the nightingale's song and the scent of roses in springtime; sometimes we are taken through gardens filled with the sorrow of winter. At times challenging, at other times comforting, they are pathways on the inner journey of the soul that open doors to unimaginable wonders, drawing back branches to reveal hidden secrets.

Rumi's Beloved has many gardens; some are visible, some are shrouded in mystery. As we wend our way in and out of these gardens, Rumi takes us through the shattering pain of separation and longing on a journey of bewilderment. His poems weave an intricate web between our image of ourselves and our innermost self.

Rumi: Gardens of the Beloved is a collection of 150 quatrains, selected from the *Divan*, that depict the delicate stages of our spiritual journey. In ever-changing shades of darkness and light along the way, we are carried on the wings of his words to the safe place of no-place. Rumi has been a source of inspiration for centuries. His poetry is all-inclusive, transcending all forms to reach the realm of essence. Rumi opens our inner eye and pierces our heart with the light of Truth. Only then do we see that we are merely '... a brush in the hand of the Master Painter'.

The Soul is Our Guide

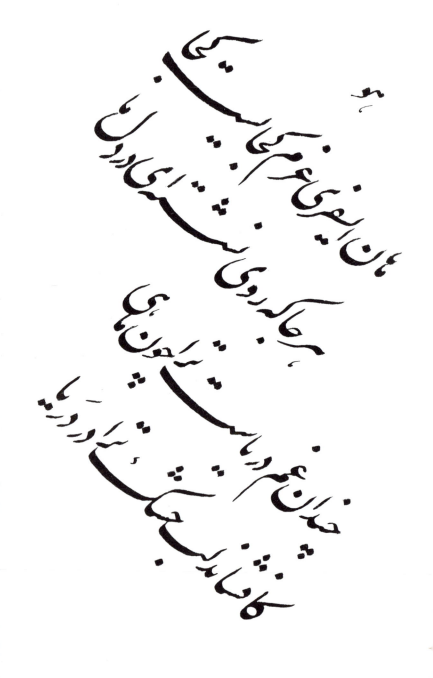

Where are you going my dear traveller,

longing for the sea like a fish?

You are in my heart wherever you go,

only that sea can quench your thirst.

Do not be idle, you will either eat

or sleep too much.

When you hear the music

of the whirling lovers, leap

and join their circle.

Indulging in our pride we keep chasing

after every fleeting image.

How strange that, being nothing,

we cultivate such grand illusions!

When you stop admiring yourself

and let the eyes of the heart

open your vision to vast other worlds

then all you do, will become admirable.

The secret of Truth is not unravelled

by questioning or giving away

your wealth and position.

You cannot exalt the heart with mere words,

pain is the price that the heart has to pay.

One needs to be strong

to bear the burning pain of longing;

rushing towards Union is not the answer.

It is in the state of separation that

all one's strength is needed.

No one could solve my dilemma

nor could they tell me where I come from.

Now, lost at the crossroads

my heart bleeds, wondering

which way is home.

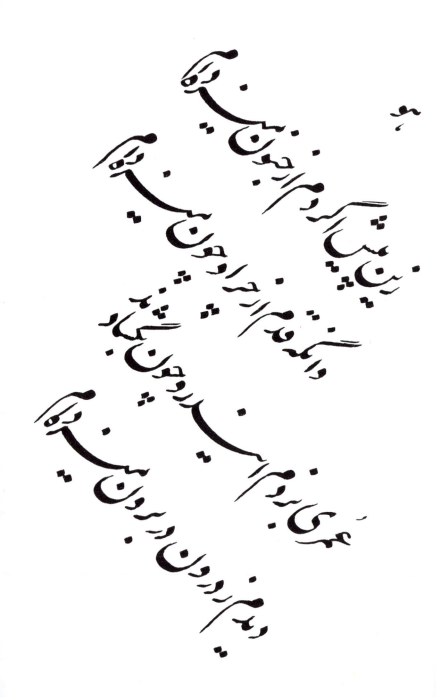

Troubled by questions all my life,

like a madman I have been

knocking at the door.

It opened!

I had been knocking from inside.

You brought release to the tormented

and offered the cup of joy to the sorrowful,

but they have long forgotten.

Tell me, if you are not to offer them the cup again,

what were you trying to teach them?

You come late to those lost in love
but when you do, you come with all your might;
gentle as a deer or regal as a lion,
but never without your piercing sword.

Sometimes you turn a deaf ear to my pleas,

and do not allow me even to kiss your feet.

It matters not if you drown or burn me,

for You are my ultimate Master.

Ever since you fled from my embrace

no one has seen me without tears.

You are always in my heart and soul;

I hope you, too, will not forget me.

Oh how lonely it is out on God's sea

with no shore in sight!

We, like ships and clouds in the night,

navigate only by the grace of His light.

I filled the garden with candles tonight,

set the table with wine and sweets

and called the musicians.

How I wish that you could be here!

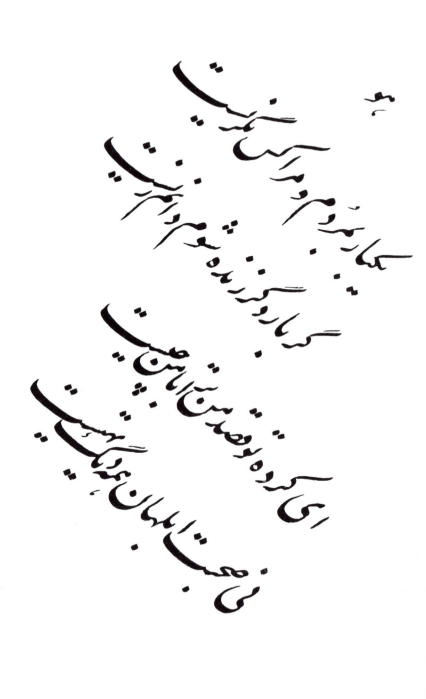

I died once but no one shed a tear,

so if I live again I will know how to be.

You pursue me with your ignorant talk

which to me sounds so empty.

Time will silence the clamour of pride
that fills the head of every man.
The wolf of nothingness
will tear the flock apart
and the flood of death
will carry everything away.

Who can uplift our soul?

The One who gave us life, the King

who at times covers the eyes of his falcon

and at times lifts the hood and looses it to its prey.

It is said that God's light

comes from six directions.

"From where?" asks the crowd,

turning left and right.

If only you could look neither way

for a moment.

A cave is hidden within you

and beyond it, unimaginable wonders.

Everybody has a job and a lover but

the hidden Lover is the most wondrous.

When life ends we are given another.

Love is the water of Eternal Life;

when you enter that immense sea,

you will know that each drop of it

brims with Life.

My heart, on this path words are hollow.

At the door of Union

you have to surrender yourself.

You will never soar to the sky

where His birds fly

unless you give up your wings.

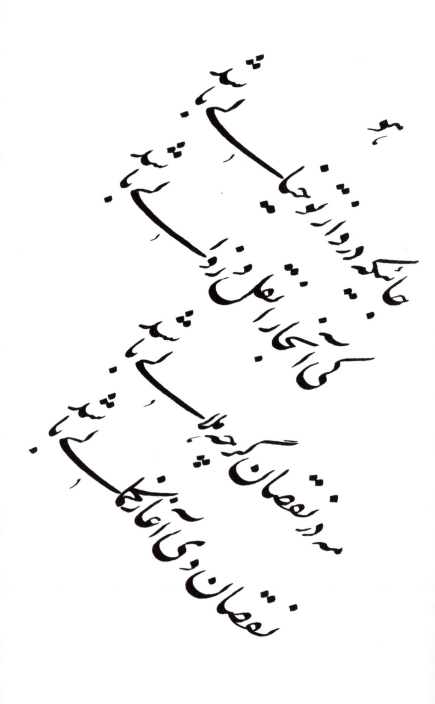

A soul that carries your image, beloved

never withers nor fades.

The slim crescent of the moon signals

only the beginning of fullness.

My dear soul, flee from the worthless,

stay close only to those with a pure heart.

Like attracts like.

A crow will lead you to the graveyard,

a parrot to a lump of sugar.

The wisdom of Truth manifests suddenly

but only in a heart that is aware.

The King does not appear unless

one is emptied of the self.

I said, "Show me what to do."

He said, *Die.*

I said, "The water has turned into oil."

He said, *Die.*

I said, "I will become a butterfly

circling around your light."

He said, *Die.*

I will never allow myself

to be the object of your mockery,

treacherous ones!

My contempt can bring such devastation

that you may never recover.

You came suddenly and stole
three things from me:
the patience from my heart,
the colour from my face
and the sleep from my eyes.
Oh, I bless the hand that
no mind can conceive!

You come from the celestial spheres
but, seduced by this clay form
you believe you belong to the earth.
Why have you forsaken that
which is your essence?

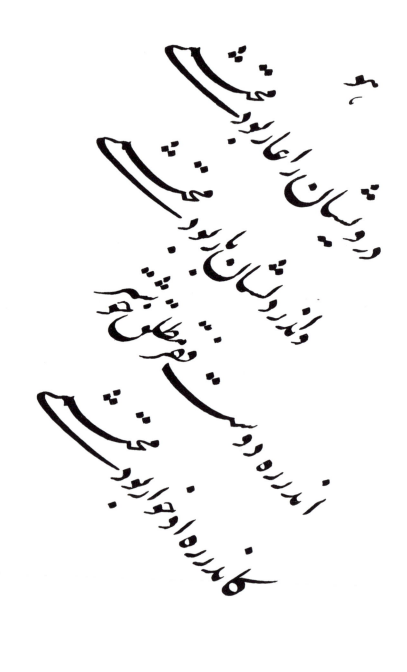

Prosperity and rank

are a heavy burden for a dervish.

In his practice of absolute poverty

he beholds the greatness of the Beloved.

To dance is not to jump to your feet at once

and rise painlessly in the air like dust.

To rise above both worlds

is to dance in the blood of your pain

and give up your life.

It is your desires that lure you further away

from your quest for the Beloved.

If you are seeking Union,

you must enter the garden of longing.

Although the road is never ending

take a step and keep walking,

do not look fearfully into the distance.

On this path let the heart be your guide

for the body is hesitant and full of fear.

We are in love with Love

because Love is our salvation.

Our guide is the Soul

and Love, the water of life.

Woe to him who cannot find the source

for his path is barred by his own ignorance.

You stepped on the ground

and the earth, pregnant with joy,

gave birth to infinite blossoms.

The cheering spread up to heaven!

The moon glanced amazed at the stars.

The two worlds we imagine
are just a dwelling place
from which we come and go.
The many stories
we have heard about the soul
are just fairy tales.

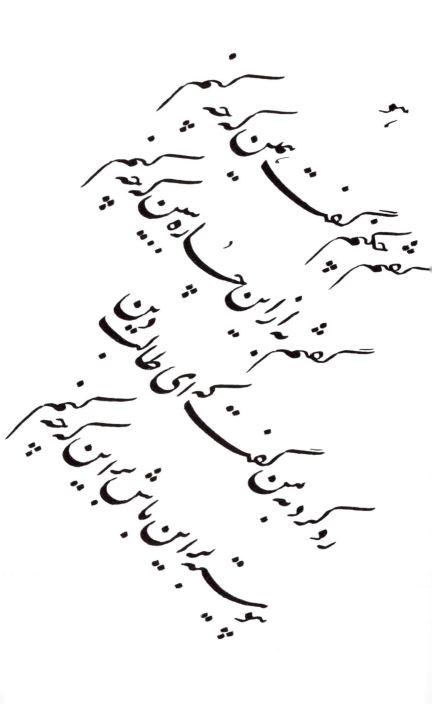

I asked, "What should I do?"

He said, *That is the question.*

I said, "Is this all you can say?"

He said, *Seeker, always keep asking,*

"What should I do?"

Do not fear, there is always wine

if you are thirsty for love.

Do not fear, there is always water

if your lips are parched.

Do not fear your ruin, inside you

there is a treasure.

Open your eyes, for this world

is only a dream.

We have stolen the moonlight
and brought it into the garden
to shake the sleep off the flowers.
Wake up, our ship has been ice-bound
long enough, the time has come
to sail the open seas.

Stay under the shadow of the lovers

for the glare of the sun will burn you up.

Stay close to them and under their protection

one day, like the sun, you will begin to shine.

In the darkness of the night
You pitched the tent of the moon
and sprinkled water
on the face of wisdom as it slept.
You promised everyone relief, yet
with the sword of longing
You struck off the head of sleep.

Sleep, my friend, but if you do
the light of Truth will slip by you unnoticed.
Asleep in the darkness of the night
you will miss the splendour of the dawn.

My heart, if you want to sit by a thorn,

what can I do?

If you do not want to pick flowers

what can I do?

If you do not see His beauty

illuminating the world,

what can I do?

Love promises

that if you give one life

you will receive thousands in return.

Listen carefully

for it is Love's way

pulling you by the ear

closer to herself.

Your body is woven

from the light of heaven.

Are you aware

that its purity and swiftness

is the envy of the angels

and its courage

keeps even devils away.

Days and nights
I have spent in hope,
Your face has never left me.
Now that my life has passed
my hope will outlive me.

Everyone has someone:

a friend, a lover, some skill or work.

But I am alone

with the dream of my Beloved

hidden in the corner of my heart.

When the wine of love is fermenting,

each night we are drawn to the tavern

to sit amongst the lovers,

for it is only they who will recognise us.

My heart,

do not let the rust of sorrow near you,

do not waste time in superficial company.

When you become satisfied with little

you will belittle the world.

Where is the moon that never rises nor sets?

Is the spirit within or without?

Stop this nonsense and let us speak straight!

The whole world is Him but tell me,

where are your eyes?

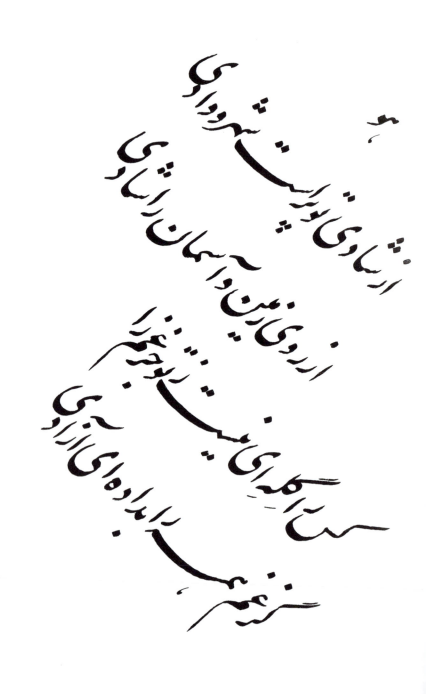

دلم ای دوست گرفتار غمت خواهد بود

پیش از این نیز مرا با تو سر و کاری بود

اشک را بر رخ من راه ده ای دل که هنوز

در میان گل و خار این دل دیوانه من

Joy has taken over the entire town,

even the sky and the earth are in bliss.

Only sorrow is complaining

because You have freed

everyone from it.

I Threw
My Heart
to the
Winds

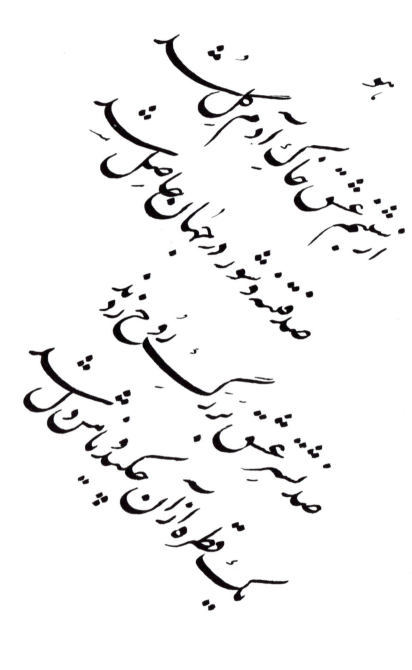

The dew of love

turned a lump of clay into a man

and the whole world was stirred.

A hundred lances pierced

the veins of Spirit;

one drop fell on Earth

and we named it Heart.

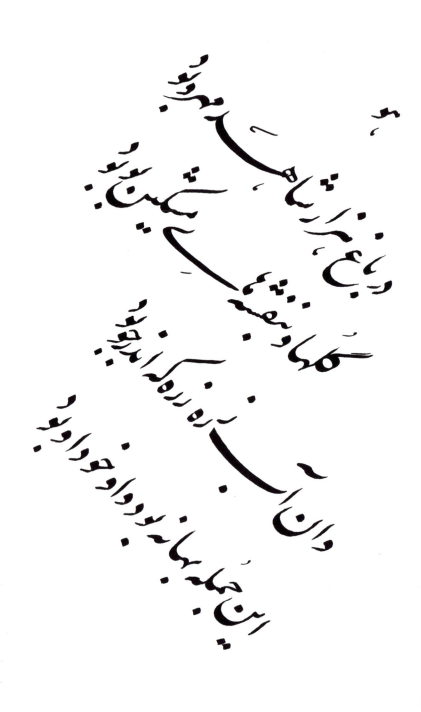

به صحرا بنگرم صحرا ته وینم
به دریا بنگرم دریا ته وینم

به هر جا بنگرم کوه و در و دشت
نشان از قامت رعنا ته وینم

A thousand beauties fill the garden:

the scent of roses,

the murmur of water

gently flowing in the stream …

But how can one describe

the indescribable?

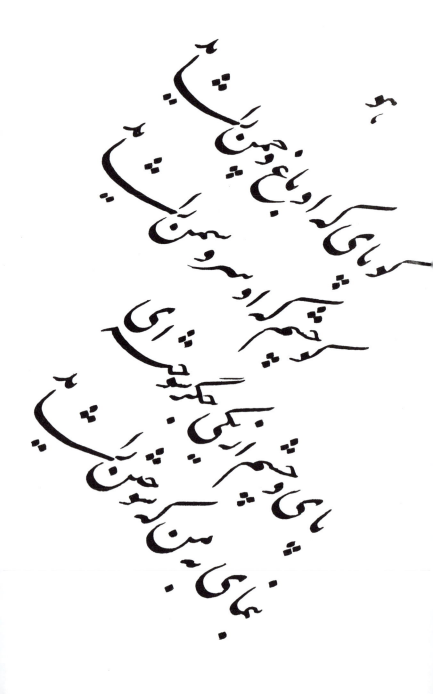

Whose feet are worthy

to enter the garden?

Whose eyes are worthy

of the cypress and the jasmine?

The feet and eyes of a heart

that has been broken.

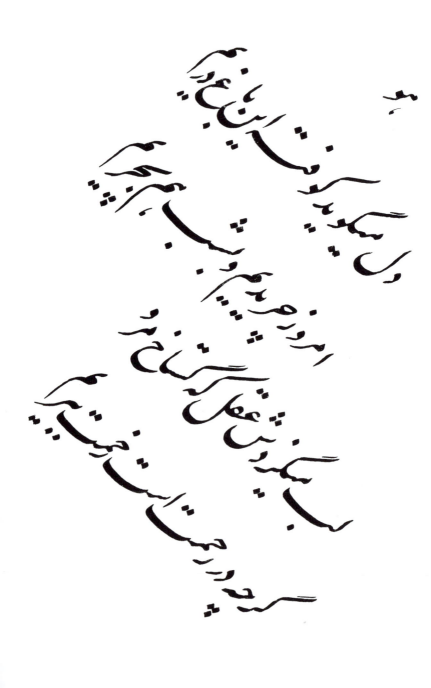

My heart rushes into the garden,

joyfully tasting all the delights.

But reason frowns, disapproving

of the heart's bad manners.

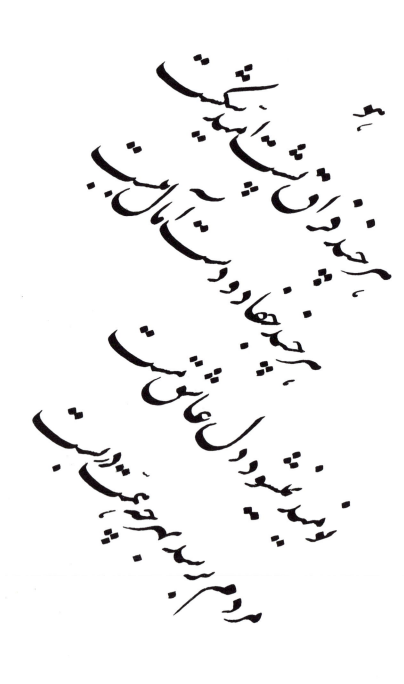

The back of hope

is bent by separation,

the hands of longing

tied by cruelty

but the lover never despairs.

For a committed heart

everything is possible.

Do not leave me,

hide in my heart like a secret,

wind around my head like a turban.

"I come and go as I please,"

you say, "swift as a heartbeat."

You can tease me as much as you like

but never leave me.

Why does sorrow turn around the heart?

Do sad and cold hearts attract it?

For a loving heart is an immense sea,

with waves that make

the tallest domes whirl.

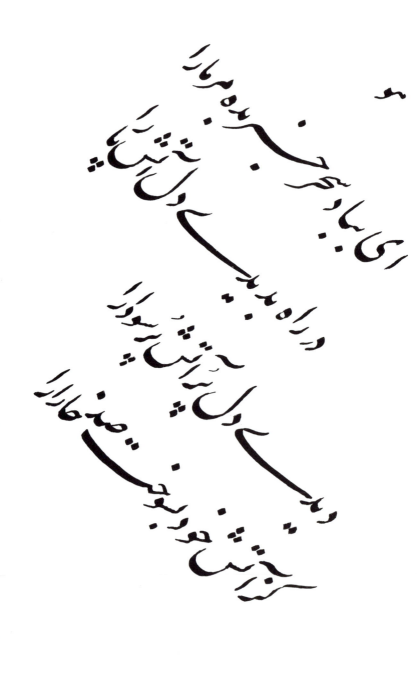

۲

ای مرغ سحر عشق ز پروانه بیاموز

کان سوخته را جان شد و آواز نیامد

این مدعیان در طلبش بی‌خبرانند

کان را که خبر شد خبری باز نیامد

Tell the morning breeze
that you have seen my fiery heart.
Tell her that my heart's passion
has burned all the thorns on my path.

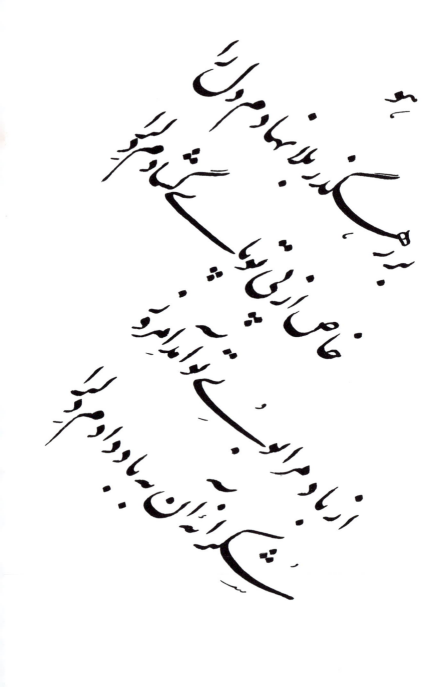

I threw my heart to the winds
and followed you.
One day the wind brought me your scent,
my heart swelled in gratitude
and scattered in the wind.

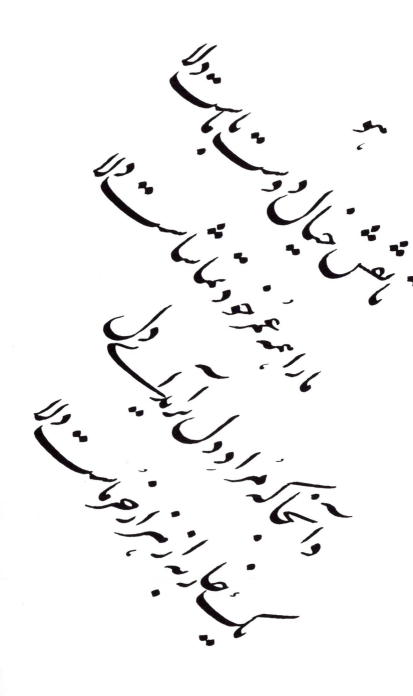

I could spend a lifetime

delighting in the image of the Friend.

But once my heart beholds the Friend,

then pain becomes more precious

than a thousand delights.

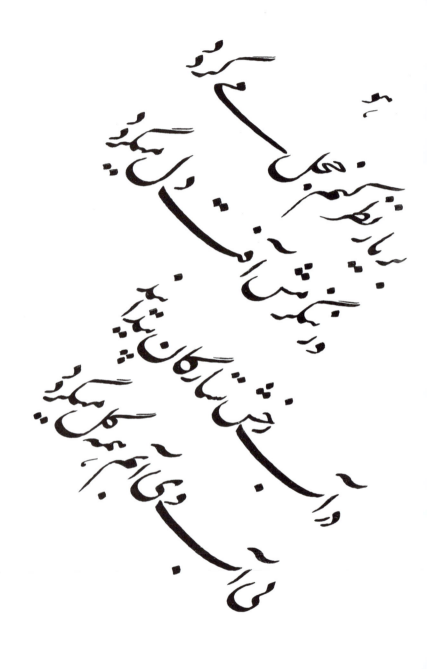

If I gaze at my beloved
she may feel embarrassed
and if I do not,
she will feel neglected.
I can see the stars reflecting
in the calm water of her face
but if I look away
I lose my clarity.

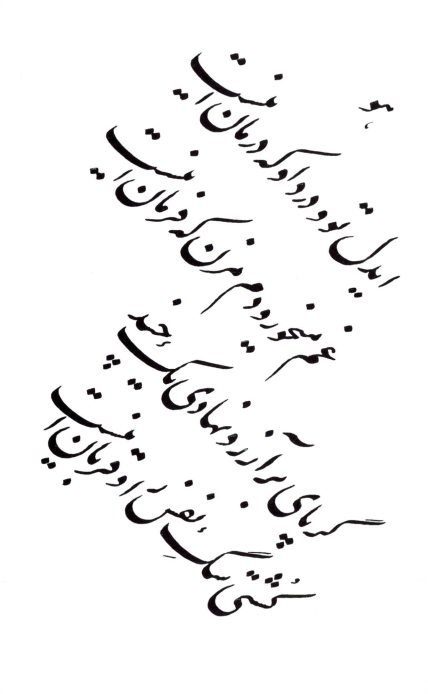

Bear the pain of longing silently, my heart

for this is the cure.

The ultimate sacrifice is to curb your desires

and surrender the ego.

My body, like a cup, holds my heart

and my thoughts are like the young wine.

Knowledge is only a trap.

How do I know?

I received this message from the Heart.

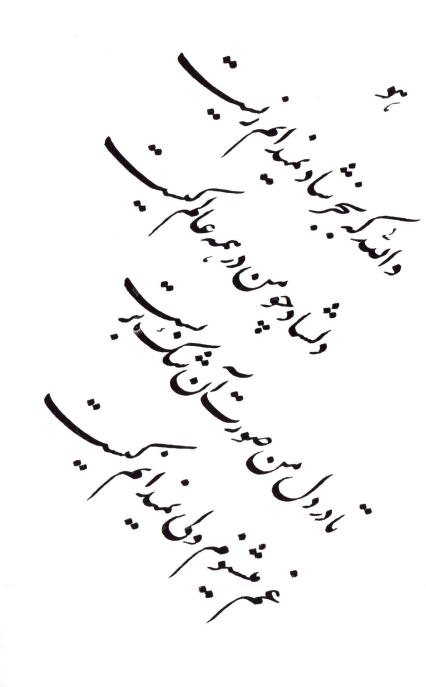

دلا دیدی که آن فرزانه فرزند

چه دید اندر خم این طاق رنگین

به جای شیر دل در بازوی داشت

به تیر آفت ایام بنشست

چه نیکو گفت آن بلبل که بگریست

که ای آزادگان این کهنه بستان

The treasure I hold in my heart

is the envy of all.

I swear to God

no one could be more joyous than me!

I hear about sorrow

but it means nothing to me.

Yesterday the nightingale was singing

a beautiful song by the stream:

"You could make a rose

out of rubies, emeralds and gold

but would it have a scent?"

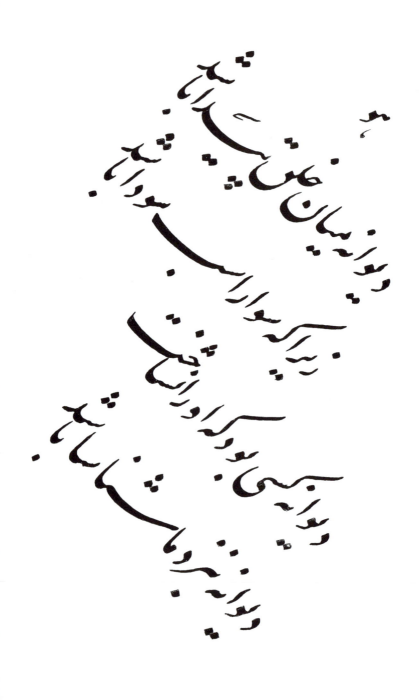

To the crowd

the dishevelled lover

riding on the horse of passion

is a madman.

But the truly mad ones

are those who are unable

to perceive him.

We may know who we are or we may not.

We may be Muslims, Jews or Christians

but until our hearts

become the mould for every heart

we will see only our differences.

I will not give up this pain so easily,
I will not give up this longing until I live.
Remembering Him is the sweetest pain
that I will not exchange for any cure.

To live without you

is to be robbed of love

and what is life without it?

To live without you

is death to me, my love

but some call it life.

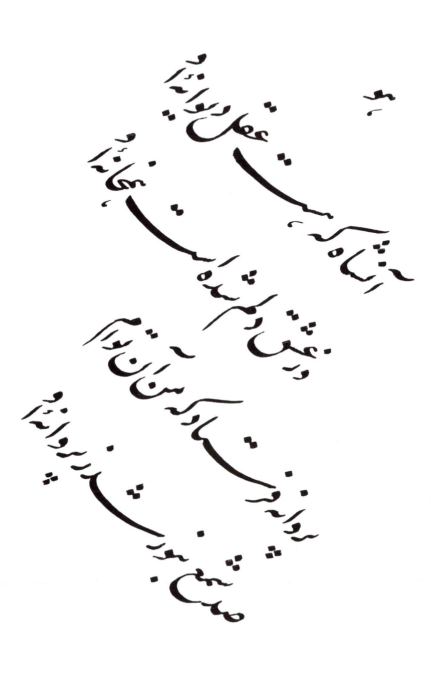

The King who stole my heart

sent a message with a butterfly.

It said, "I am yours"

and a hundred candles

burst into flame.

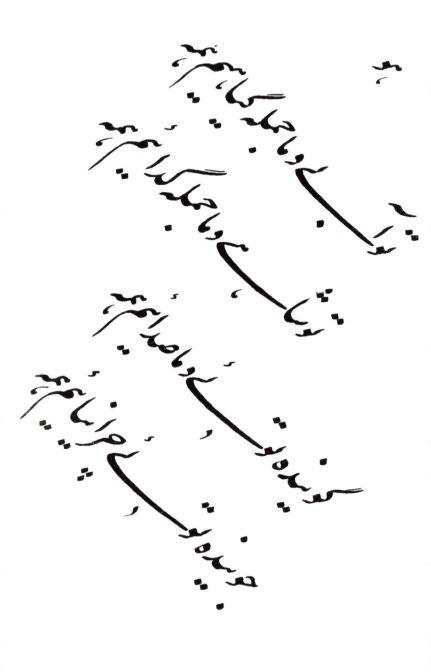

You are Water,

we are the thirsty plants,

You are the King,

we are the beggars at the gate,

You are the Speaker,

we are Your voice.

How could we not

answer Your call?

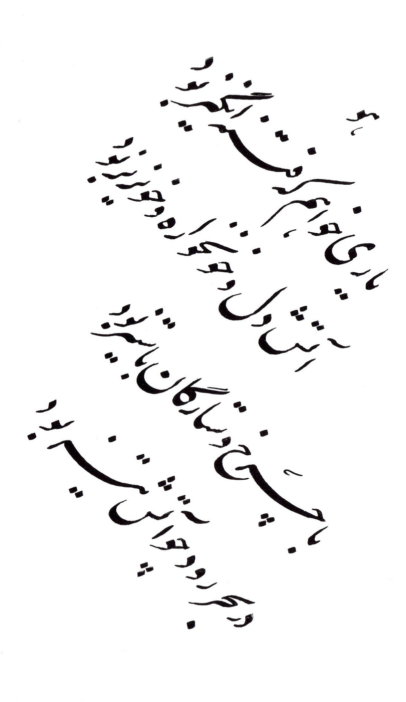

I want a lover with a fiery heart,

at war with the world and the stars;

a lover not afraid of bloodshed or murder,

and whose fire no water can quench.

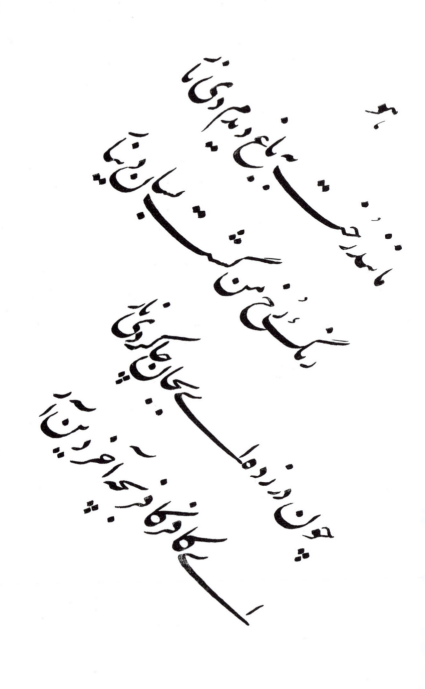

The pomegranate I saw yesterday

with the colour of your radiant face

set me on fire

and turned my face ashen and grey.

How do you expect me to trust you?

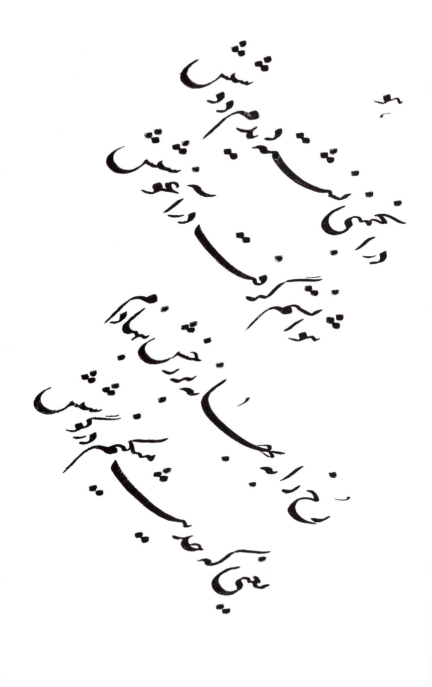

Last night in a gathering
I caught a glimpse of my beloved.
Too embarrassed to embrace him
I put my face against his cheek
pretending to whisper
something in his ear.

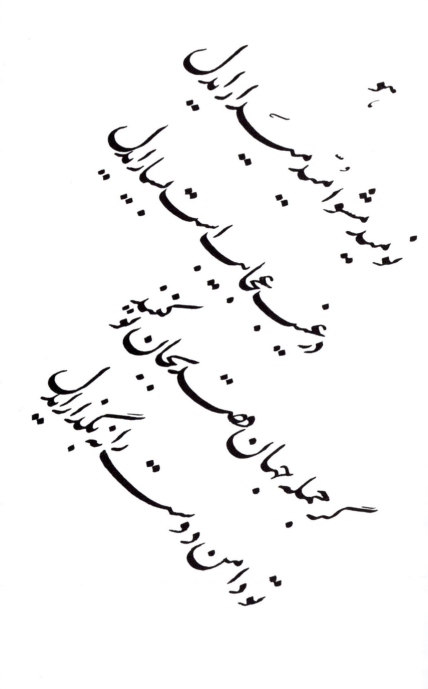

Never lose hope, my heart,

miracles dwell in the invisible.

If the whole world turns against you

keep your eyes on the Friend.

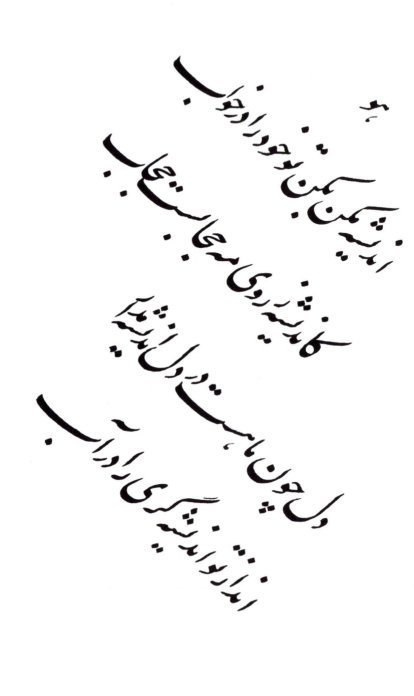

Put your thoughts to sleep,

do not let them cast a shadow

over the moon of your heart.

Let go of thinking.

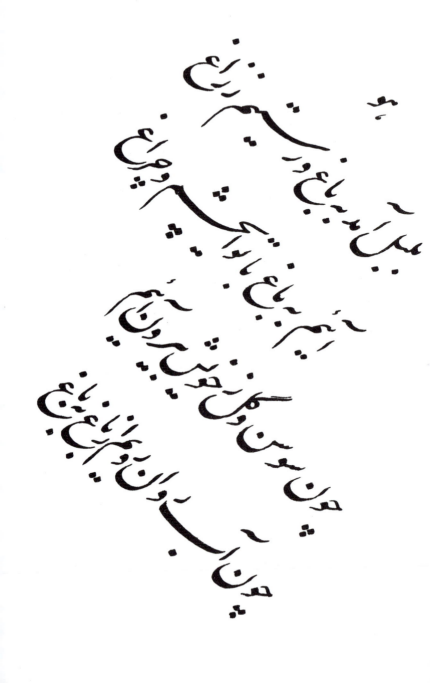

Light of my eyes
the nightingale has returned.
We will lose ourselves in the garden
and come out in blossom
like the lilies and roses;
we will become water and flow
from garden to garden.

I am whirled into ecstasy!

The drunken nightingale sings in my ear.

I hear your luring voice in the wind,

your image sparkles on the water,

the delicate scent in the air

is so familiar ...

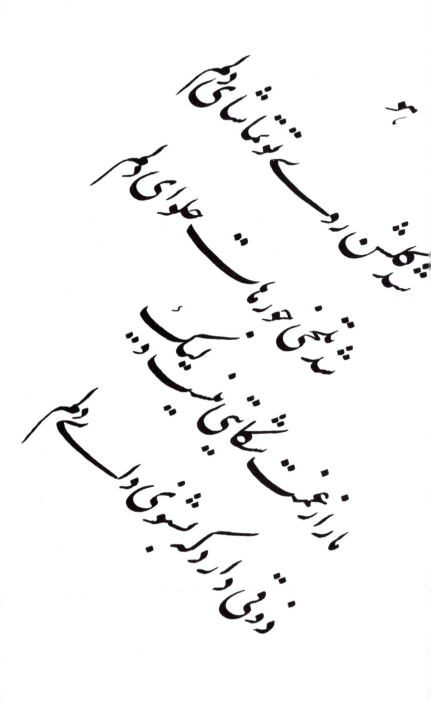

۳

چشم دل باز کن که جان بینی
آنچه نادیدنی است آن بینی

گر به اقلیم عشق روی آری
همه آفاق گلستان بینی

بر همه اهل آن زمین به مراد
گردش دور آسمان بینی

آنچه بینی دلت همان خواهد
وآنچه خواهد دلت همان بینی

Is your face a beautiful blossom

or a sweet torture?

I have no complaints

but my heart is tempted

to let you

hear of its sorrows.

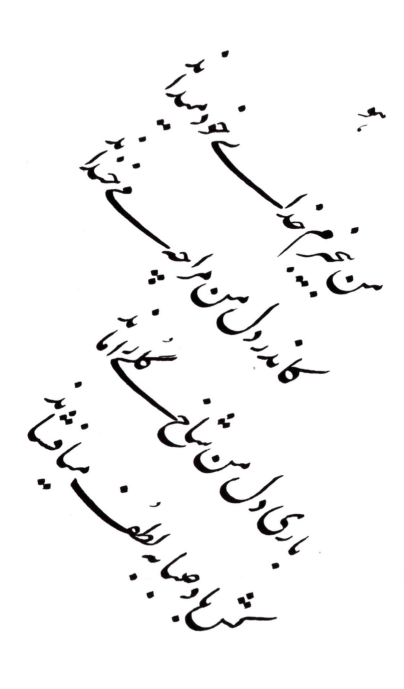

God only knows

what this joy, this laughter

bubbling inside my heart, could be!

Maybe the playful wind is scattering

the rose petals of my heart.

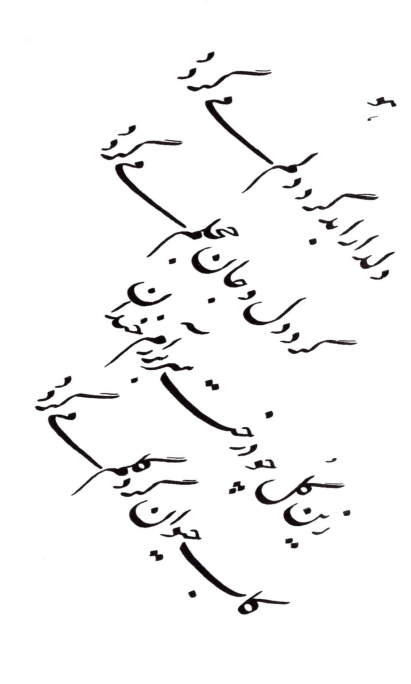

Eternal Love turns incessantly

around my humbled heart

and, smiling,

I will rise from the ground

like a tree

because the water of life

turns incessantly

around me.

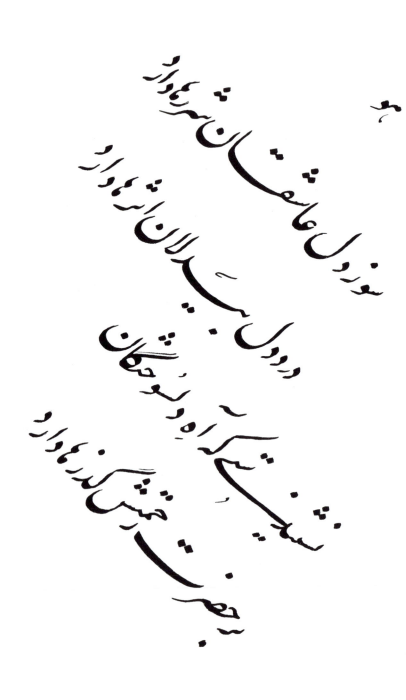

A special spark rises

from the sorrow of a burning heart.

Have you ever heard

how the sigh of a broken heart

touches the Beloved?

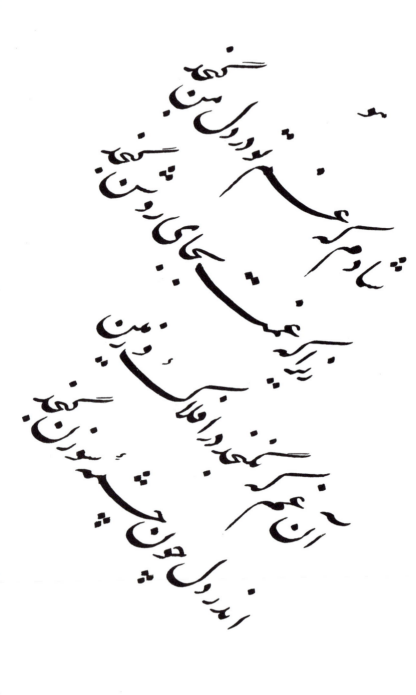

I am delighted

that my heart welcomes sorrow

for the sorrow

that the earth and the sky

can not behold

is contained in a heart

as small

as the eye of a needle.

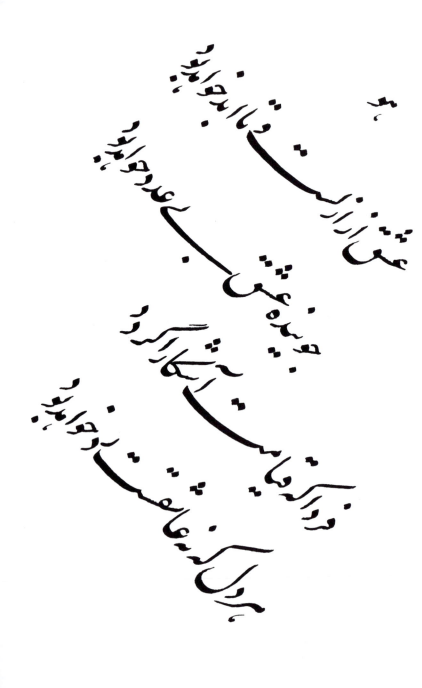

Love was from the beginning of time
and love will be for all eternity.
On the day of resurrection
the heart devoid of love will not pass
through the gate.

I have become insane and bewildered,

take my hand.

Even the most unworthy have a friend,

I am lost without You.

Take my hand!

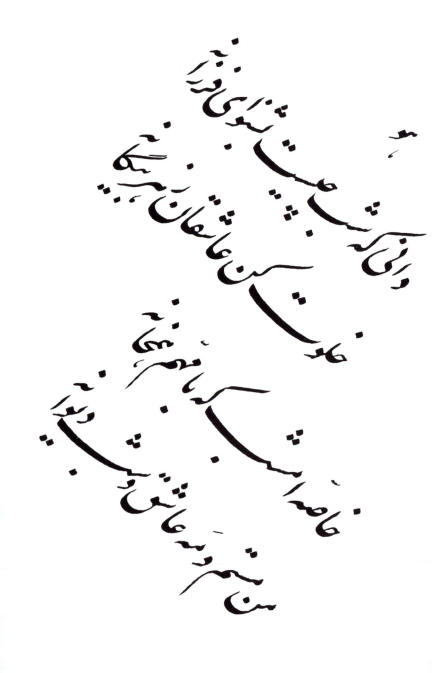

Do you know, knower,

what the night is?

It is the sanctuary of lovers.

On this glorious night

I am drunk with the moon.

The moon has fallen in love

and the night has gone mad.

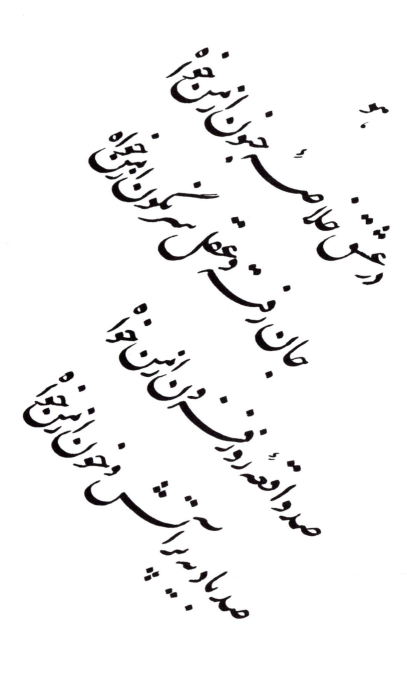

In love, ask for madness,
a life abandoned and a mind lost,
ask for dangerous adventures
in deserts filled with blood and fire!

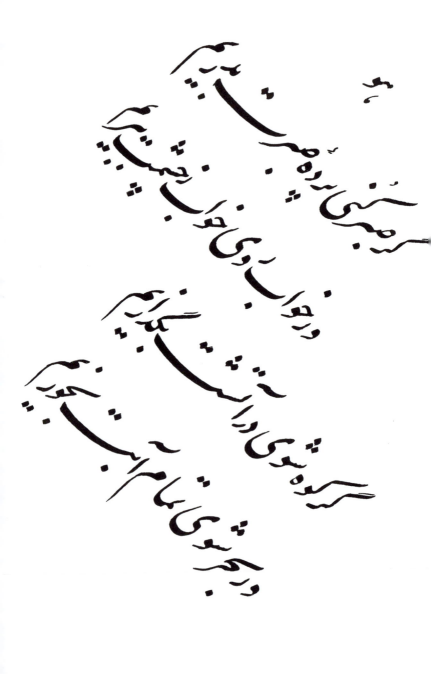

Hesitate

and I will tear apart your patience.

Fall asleep

and I will snatch the sleep from your eyes.

Become a mountain

and I will set it on fire.

Become an ocean

and I will drink all its water.

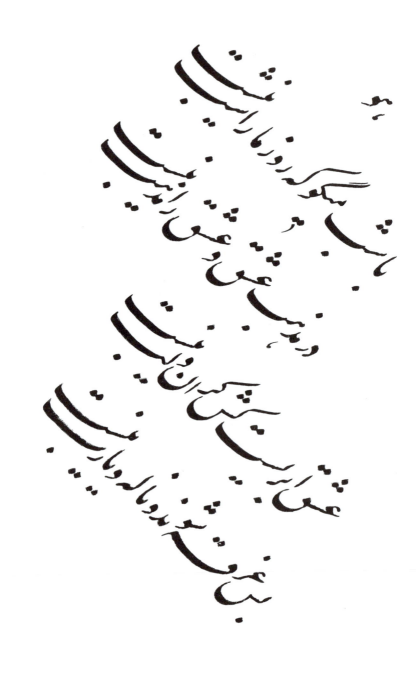

Lover, tell the night

that your day

will never end in its arms.

The religion of Love

is a sea without a shore

where lovers drown

without a sigh,

without a cry.

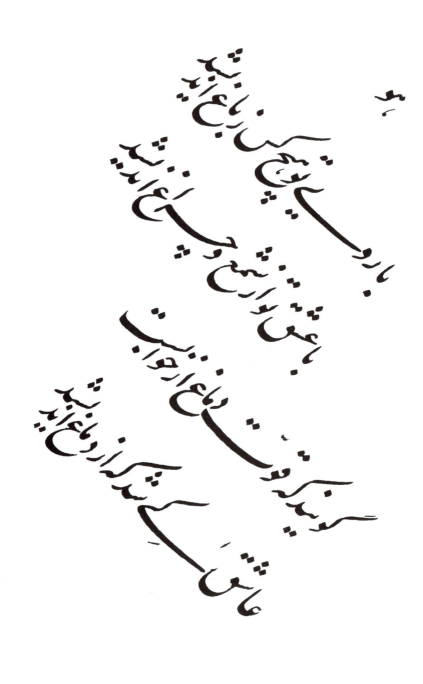

Would I think of gardens, beloved,

with your face by my side?

Would I long for light, beloved,

when I am lit by the fire of your love?

They say sleep strengthens the mind

but does a lover need a mind?

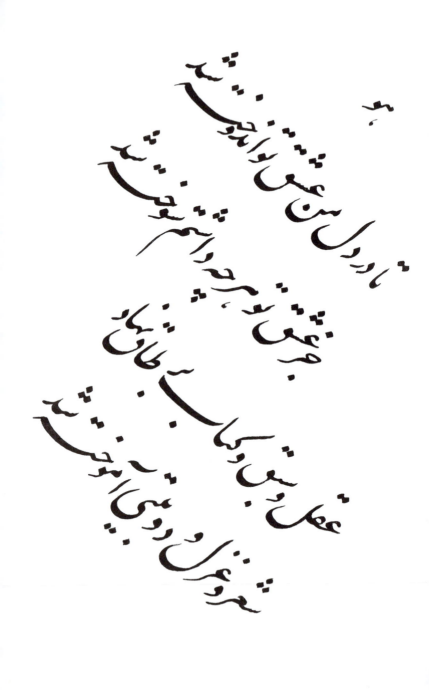

نگارا بر منِ بی دل نظر کن

خدا را حال زارِ من نظر کن

به چشمِ مرحمت بر من نظر کن

چو رحم آید تو را بر من نظر کن

چنین بی رحم تا کی دل شکستن

نظر کن گاه گاهی سوی ما هم

The fire of Love blazed in my heart
and consumed everything.
My books, my erudition and my mind
I put away on a shelf.
Now I only write poems.

In the kitchen of love
only the beautiful are killed.
Death does not frighten a true lover
for those not dying for love
are already corpses.

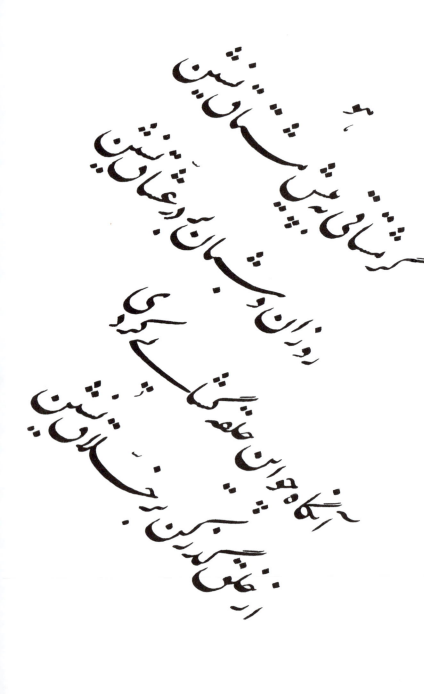

When you are taken by Love

sit day and night

at the door of the enchanted lovers.

Once you have unlocked

the mystery in their circle

you may pass beyond the created

and sit at the door of the Creator.

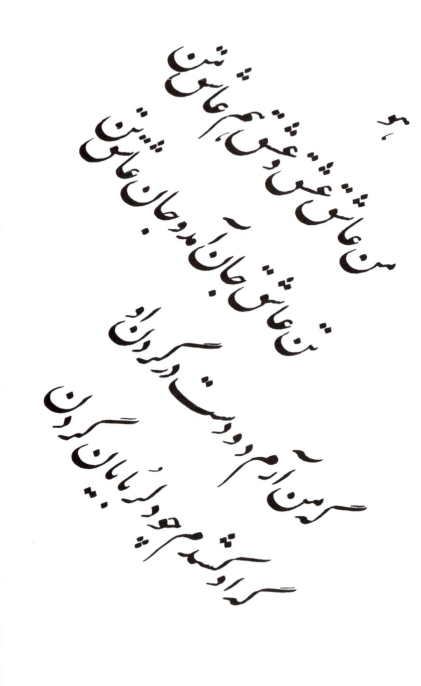

I am in love with Love and Love

is in love with me.

My body is in love with the soul

and the soul

is in love with my body.

I opened my arms to Love

and Love embraced me

like a lover.

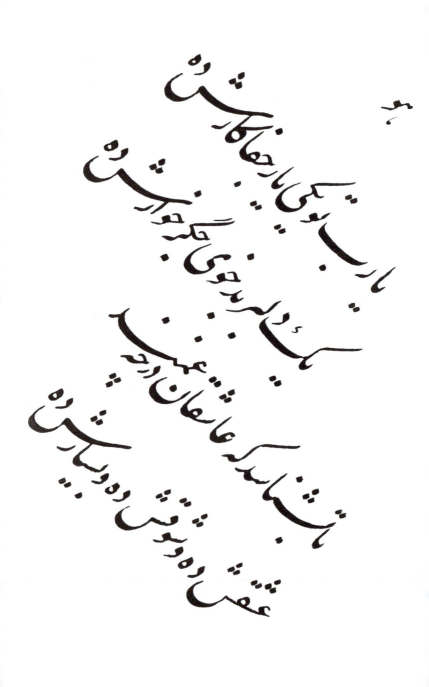

Oh God, give them a cruel lover,

let them be consumed with passion

for someone ill-tempered and bloodthirsty

so that they know the pain a true lover feels!

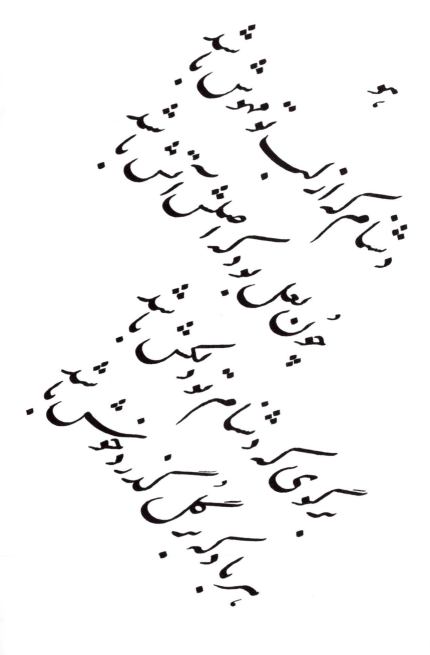

From your lips

scorn is as beautiful as the ruby

holding fire in its essence.

From your lips

scorn is as gentle as the breeze

caressing the flowers.

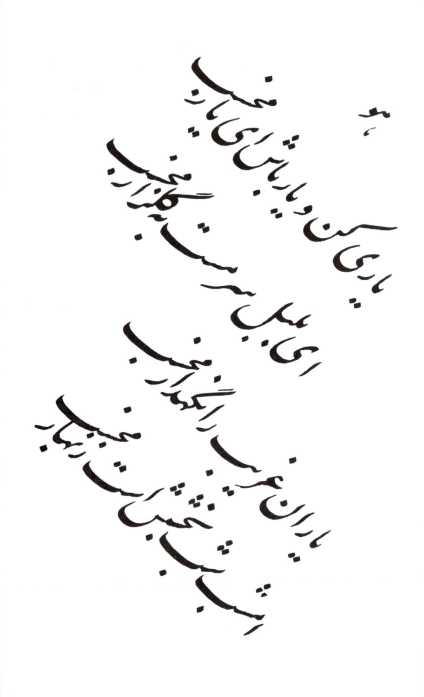

Do not desert me,

be my friend, my help, beloved.

Be my enchanting nightingale, my garden.

Do not abandon your lonely friend.

Tonight the night is generous and merciful,

do not desert me!

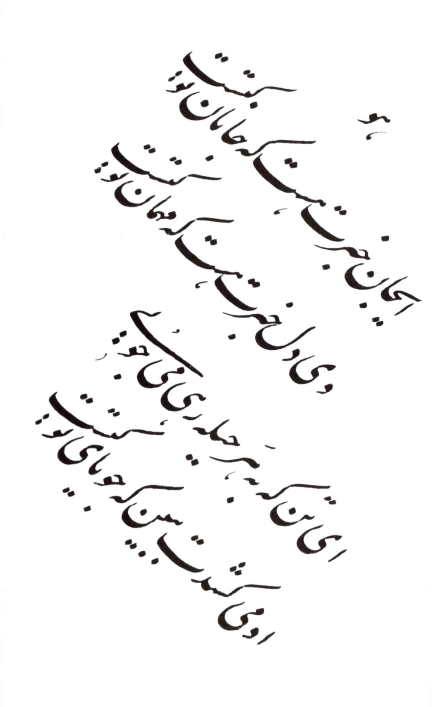

My spirit

know and behold the eternal Spirit.

My heart

know and honour your Guest.

My body

know that no trick will save you from

the One

who seeks you.

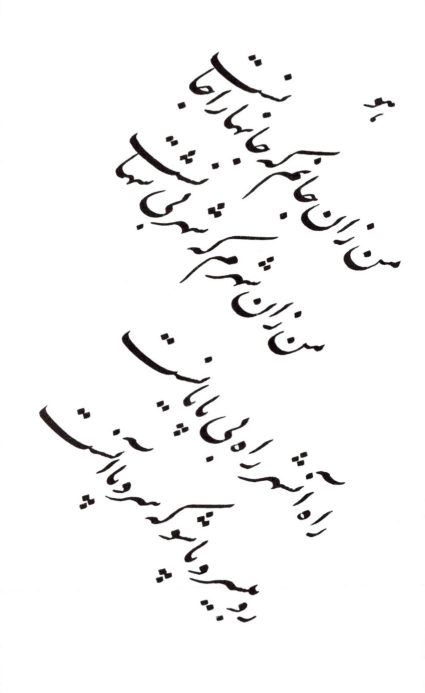

I know that my spirit belongs

to the Spirit of all Spirit.

I know I belong to the city

of those who have no place.

But to find my way there

I need to let go of my knowing.

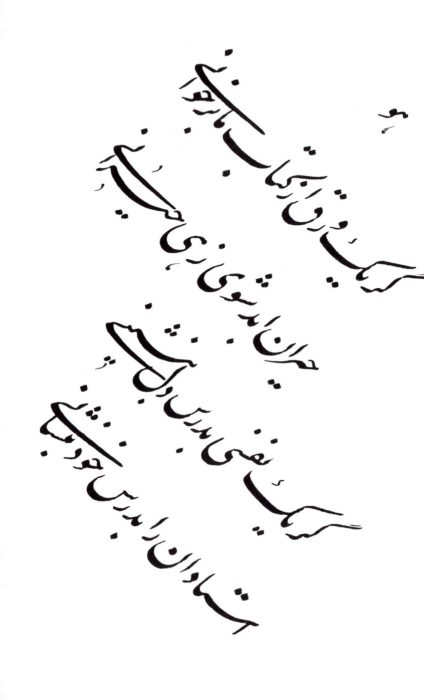

One page of our book

will leave you bewildered for ever.

One real moment at the feet of the Heart

will turn your teachers into pupils.

Spirit is
Never Tired
of Lovers

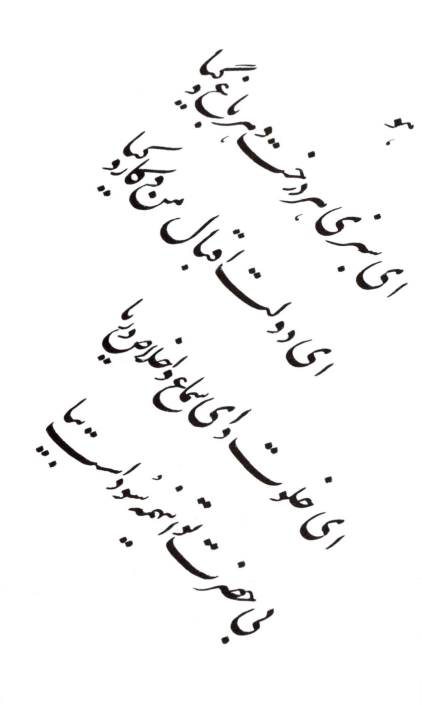

The green in every tree

is You.

The beauty of every garden

is You.

My wealth, my work, my master

is You.

Solitude, purity, pretence

is You.

There is no reality

but You.

The one You have exalted
never falls from grace.
Even the heavens bend
to kiss the feet
that You have chained.

When my soul soared
to that blessed sphere
I was free of the tyranny
of "why?" and "how?"
At last
the thousand veils lifted
and I could behold
the hidden secret.

Love came rushing

like blood in my veins

and emptied me of myself.

Now, filled with the Beloved,

I have only a name.

You are the divine word,

you mirror the majesty of the King.

All the world is contained in you.

What you are seeking is within.

O tulip, learn about colour from my face;
O Venus, learn from my heart how to play the lute.
O Destiny, when the trumpet of union sounds
come and learn about music.

A pure heart, open to the Light
will be filled with the elixir of Truth.
You may see my body
but I am only a grain of salt
dissolved in the sea of Love.

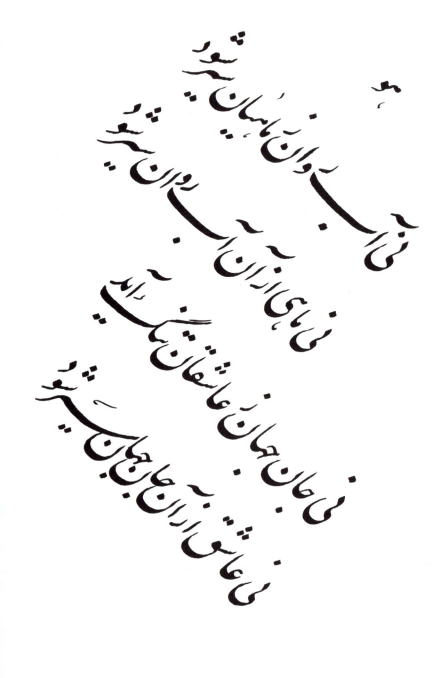

Water never tires of fish

nor do fish ever tire of water.

Spirit is never tired of lovers

nor lovers of Spirit.

We have spirit,

but what does Spirit have?

Bread feeds the hungry

but what feeds bread?

In life, anything can be exchanged

except the source of life itself.

Our horse flew on the wings of love

from the land of nothingness

and our night became illuminated

with the wine of Union.

From that wine our lips will never dry

and morning will never come.

I drank from the water of life
and all disease vanished.
I entered the garden of Union
and I found no thorns.
They say there is a doorway
from heart to heart
but what is the use of a door
when there are no walls?

Love, You are my Certainty.

You are the Creator and I, the created.

Cover the eyes of the jealous ones

when You lift me to the stars.

Today, amazed and bewildered
I have shut the door on thought
and turned to music.
There are a hundred ways
to kneel and pray
at the altar of the Beloved.

Beyond belief and disbelief
lies the vast expanse of ecstasy
where the mystic lays his head
on the cushion of Truth.

"Write me a verse," I said.

He was offended.

What can I reveal in a line or two?

"Then choose a verse for me to recite." I said.

Which verse do you think could contain me?

In the beginning

we made a special agreement

to come here

but this world of matter

is not our home.

A man may pride himself on his piety

but beyond his prayers and piety

there is another world.

When my pain became the cause of my cure

my contempt changed into reverence

and my doubt into certainty.

I see that I have been the veil on my path.

Now my body has become my heart

my heart has become my soul

and my spirit, the eternal Spirit.

There is a loneliness more precious than life.

There is a freedom more precious than the world.

Infinitely more precious than life and the world

is that moment when one is alone with God.

I found that no joy in the world

could relieve me of my sorrows, but Him.

I wanted to tell Him so many things

but when He appeared

I could not utter a word.

Seek love, seek love

for it is the gem of your essence.

Seek the One, seek the One

for He is yours for eternity.

But forbid yourself to call Him yours

for what is yours is only

the sorrow

and the longing.

In every sphere

I see the pupil of the eye,

in every pupil

I see the whole sphere.

It is the eyes of the foolish

that see one as two

while I see every two

as one.

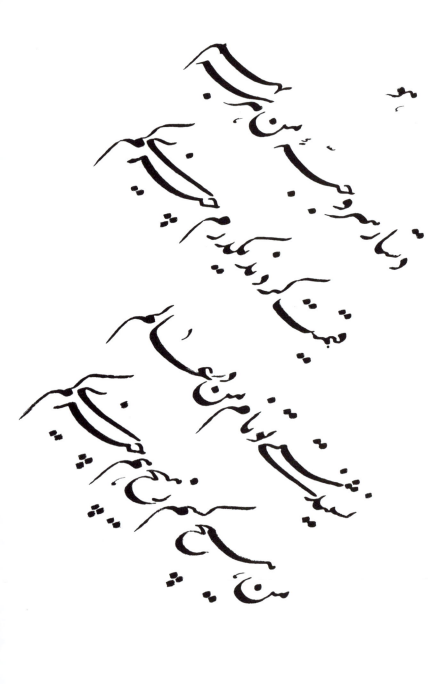

My turban, cloak and head

can be bought for less than a penny.

No one has ever heard my name.

I am nothing, nothing!

If you only knew

what bliss I find in being nothing,

you would never

advise me how to live.

When the sword of nothingness

ends my days

I will laugh at those

who mourn my death.

In Your love I grew tall;

joyous, I have risen to the skies.

They think I turn around Him

but truly I turn around Myself.

I praised you in the day

but never knew it

I slept with you at night

but never knew it

I believed I was myself

but I was You

and never knew it.

My Beloved, I do not know anymore

if I am on earth or in heaven!

Do not hand me the wine

bring it to my lips,

I am so drunk

I cannot find the way

to my mouth.

Beloved

when I look upon myself

I see that my intelligence and clarity

is You.

Everything that is precious

in my worthless being

is You.

Your Spirit dispersed the clouds

of my darkness and profanity.

Now, in the light, You sing in my heart

and dance like wine in my head.

When I walk on the path

when I enter the house of Love

I see You.

You are the King in every town.

I see You in the sun, the moon and the stars,

I see Your altar in every plant,

in every leaf.

I am bewildered by the Beloved,

He belongs to me.

Do not search elsewhere,

He lives in my heart.

I am not misleading you when I say

I am Him!

Angels dance only with You, Beloved

and only before You

do I bow in adoration.

You may accept me or not

but I will be at your feet forever.

Glorious is the man who can
distinguish the cotton of the body
from the cloth of spirit.
When Hallaj called out "I am Truth,"
it was not him who spoke,
but God!

There is another language beyond language,

another place beyond heaven and hell.

Precious gems come from another mine,

the heart draws light from another source.

In the glorious season of Union
the heart rises from the ashes
sparkling with light.
From the laughter of thunder and lightning
the clouds cry tears
that fill the garden with joy.

No one has seen

how You have risen in my chest

bright as the Moon!

No one has seen how Your Spirit

runs like blood

through my body.

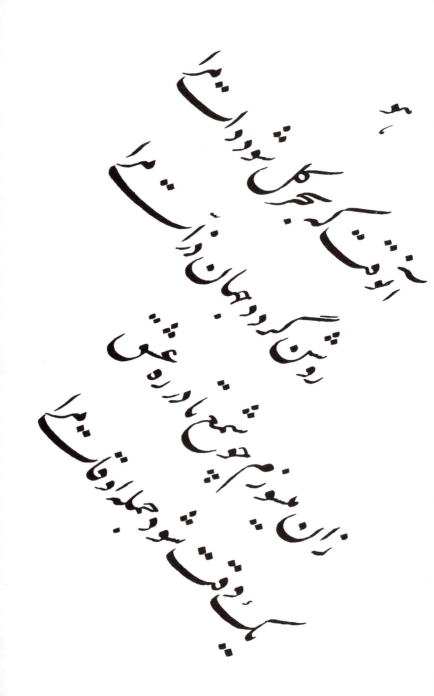

When I become the Sea

each atom flames out of me in glory.

When I am ablaze

each moment becomes Eternity.

I drank from His flaming cup
and lost my mind.
Now, like a moth, I am circling
around His Sun.

I am no longer just one drop,

I have become the entire Sea.

I speak the language of the heart

where every particle of me,

united, shouts in ecstasy!

Unless one is completely annihilated

Union is not a reality.

Union is not the merging of spirits;

the secret of Union

is the annihilation itself.

The cup I hold in my hand

is filled with the wine of Light.

It opened my eyes

and now I see the Beloved

everywhere.

The Master cut a reed from the riverbed
carved nine holes in it and called it Man.
The reed, in agony, has never stopped longing
to behold the lips that breathed into it.

What could life and the world hold
for the one who has befriended You?
In love and bewildered,
even if You offered him both worlds
what could he do with either?

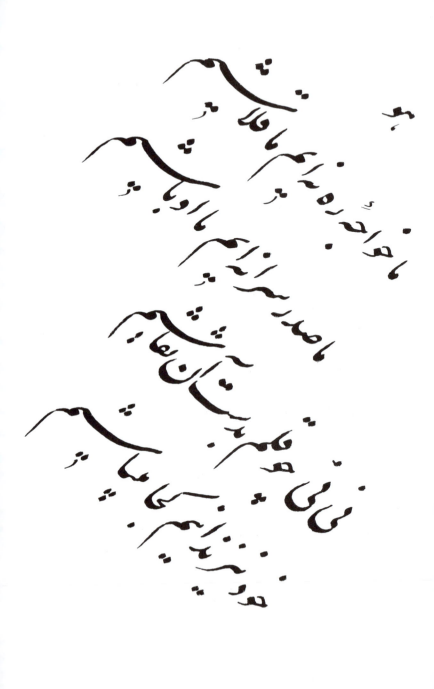

On the path of Love

we are neither masters

nor the owners of our lives.

We are only a brush

in the hand

of the Master Painter.

In His spring I blossomed,

in His garden of abundance

I drank His wine

and vanished

in the splendour

of His face.

My heart saw Love

galloping alone towards the desert

and, shattered by love's majesty,

fell in love with Love.

Around the blazing Sun

the lovers whirl like specks of dust.

In the spring breeze of love

every branch that is not dry

is dancing.

The night has passed
and still we are not sober.
In the garden of the heart
the feast goes on.
The nightingale is singing
and the lover and beloved
are entwined into one.

Oh flower, what makes you smile,

the beauty of the rose garden

or the love song of the nightingale?

Or have you suddenly seen

the hidden face of the Beloved

and recognised yourself in Him?

What passed between us

in that luminous night

can never be written or told.

On my final journey

from this world

the creases of my shroud

will unfold our story.

.

Those beautiful words we said to one another

are hidden in the secret heart of heaven.

One day, like the rain, they will pour

our love story all over the world.

Terms & Symbolism

Beloved, Friend, King	Terms used by Rumi referring to God.
Dervish	A Sufi mystic.
Drunk, Drunkenness	Intoxication with Love.
Garden	An inner space, depicting the outward beauty of nature and the inward beauty of Spirit.
Hallaj	A Sufi, accused of heresy and executed in 922 in Baghdad for his ecstatic statements such as: Ana al Haqq, "I am Truth."
Killing	Severing the attachment to the ego.
Moon	Symbol of the heart of the mystic.
Nightingale	Symbol of the soul's longing.
Poverty	The complete annihilation of the self as a key to the attainment of Union and Truth.
Rose	Symbol of the beauty of the Beloved.
Rose-garden	Paradise and eternal Beauty.
Sufi	Mystic in search of the Beloved.

The Two Worlds	Not two separate worlds but two aspects of a continuous process. The world of matter is at one end of the spectrum while the essence, invisible to the eye, is at the other end.
Veil	Symbol of layers of the ego separating the self from the Beloved.
Whirling	Sema – Spiritual dance of the Sufis.
Wine	Symbol of the ecstatic love of God.

Index

Garden of the Heart

Garden of the Spirit